Parenting is a LOVE-HATE relationship

Foreword

I hate my kids! No, really, I do, at times. Well hate is a strong word and an exaggeration however dislike may be more appropriate. If you've never found yourself sitting in a dark room, contemplating what went wrong today and how different your life would be if you hadn't had children, this book is not for you. Make faces if you like. We both know that every parent has had these moments. It's how we address the feelings that make or break what type of parent we are.

It's natural to have feelings of disdain, especially for your children. It's natural to feel like you've failed based on the way your kids behave in a moment. It's also natural to accept that you nor your children are perfect and it's okay. You see, this concept of the perfect family is a farce. Something society created to shame you into medicating then labeling your children, ultimately fueling a very unhealthy competition amongst you, other parents and children. A competition that has us lying, cheating and stealing our ways into top tier neighborhoods, clubs and schools.

Reality is much simpler than this world. Reality is the place where we accept responsibility for our homes. Where we're accountable for what works and what doesn't. Where we do our best on the front end while trusting the process on the back. Where we set the example for our children in the beginning and let maturity take care of the rest.

7 ways to keep your sanity and be a GREAT leader in your home!

MEAN WHAT YOU SAY, SAY WHAT YOU MEAN!

Obviously, my children have two parents, what's not obvious is whether they come from a two-parent home, one child does, the oldest two, do not. Well what does that mean? Really? You know! I am laughing out loud, to myself so hard right now. Let's walk through this, slowly.

My oldest two daughters are twenty and seventeen, from a previous ten-year relationship. This relationship changed the trajectory of my life and perception about love all together. I learned so much about myself and expectations that I could write fifty "31 days of" or "7 lessons learned about" books around the topic of self-love alone. We experienced poverty, generational curses, domestic abuse, cheating, drugs and more over the course of those ten years. It was like a local love and hip-hop episode with no love or hip-hop. We barely made it out alive.

Fast forward twenty child rearing years, our parenting styles are not the same. My girls have always been with me. In my house, I have always worked. I sacrificed personal intimate dating relationships during their developmental years, and I prioritized higher education. I had no idea where I wanted to take my degrees however I knew that they were required. As I sit here writing this book, I actively use both degrees in all my entrepreneurial and professional endeavors therefore that sacrifice was the right one for me. I digress. My trajectory and my image to my daughters have always been priority.

He prioritized him. It's not a dig and it's not embellishment. We were nineteen and eighteen when we got pregnant with our first daughter. He spent his teen years raising his two younger brothers. He never got the opportunity to enjoy being a child so that showed up in his parenting. He lived the life that he saw fit for him and included his daughters where they fit. They saw different things in the separate households.

As a second-year cosmetology student and a junior in high school their morals, thought processes and life views have been shaped by what they've seen and heard us say either verbally or by our actions. In most cases, our actions spoke far louder than anything we said.

My oldest daughter is creative, she's finishing up her cosmetology license and will be a premiere colorist in the hair care field; my youngest daughter is creative and an academic, she's going to write films and documentaries that will challenge the status quo by speaking truth to power. They are very different. They are also very much their parents' children.

At different points in times, both would stare you straight in your face and lie through their teeth. At different points in times they'd hide things to protect themselves and share things to manipulate situations. At different points in time they both have succumb to peer pressure and made questionable decisions that shifted the trajectory of their futures. In some cases, we'd say they sound like pretty normal teenagers. In others as we whip out the proverbial microscope, we can identify exactly who they got which action from.

My oldest daughter went through a season that prompted me to write the first text in the, "A Mother's Love" series. She had literally lost her mind.

I remember this day like it was yesterday; it was a Tuesday in January and I woke up to get ready for work. As usual I walked through my house to lay eyes on each of my children. No specific reason for it, it's just my routine. When I got to my oldest daughter's room, I noticed lumping in the bed. My daughter is petite, I mean extremely petite so the pile underneath the cover couldn't have possibly been her. After cleaning my eyes and pounding on the pile, I confirmed that my child was in fact missing. I looked for clues. I knocked on friends' doors. I texted phones. I called 911. I woke up my middle daughter. I lost it.

A few hours and police report later, I received an extremely calm text reassuring me that she was safe, at school. I won't belabor the point with the details of how horrible the experience was or what happened next. I will tell you that when I finally got a hold of her, an investigation was launched into my parenting, by the school, and our relationship got a lot worse before it got better. My daughter had reached that point where she was comparing her life to the lives of her friends. They could come and go as they pleased. Their mal behavior was rewarded with allowances and new cars. Their family secrets created an environment of do as I say, not as I do and, in some cases, do exactly what I do. Her reality was different. In her eyes, I was strict. Lame. And dead set on ruining her life. It took some time, real life experiences and transparency but she later realized that my rules and actions aligned with a life that was designed to suit her best interest, based on how well I knew her as opposed to my personal enjoyment.

For a period, I contemplated letting her go live with her father and his new family. Fortunately, life worked it so that it wasn't possible. It wasn't in her best interest. Honestly, I had serious concerns about that. However, sometimes the best lesson is learned by allowing our loved ones to experience the very thing they are seeking. I live by this!

Not too long after and some counseling sessions, we discovered what I had already known, I was right. I am not saying that to brag or boast. It's the way things played out. Her friends that she fought so hard to entertain and impress, were not her friends. They were jealous and later spread rumors about her. She was so hurt. The life that she fought so hard to live, turned its back on her. She realized that she was truly blessed in life; finishing high school, performing well at work and sticking to her consistent group of friends while nurturing her own growth were the things that would serve her best.

Life is not perfect, there's no such thing. My daughter realized that at her core, her values come from the things that she's seen over the course of her life. She had to come to that realization on her own. Change was not happening any other way. I am not the posterchild for motherhood, I have made a lot of mistakes. Some you'll read about in other chapters. I have, always been exactly who I said I was, the good, bad and ugly. I walked consistently along that truth. It's why I strongly believe that our children learn the most from what they see as opposed to what we say, unless what we say, aligns with what they see.

REFLECTIONS,
"MEAN WHAT YOU SAY, SAY WHAT YOU MEAN!"

BE CONSISTENT!

My children have a father and one stepdad. They know about one boyfriend in between the two and that relationship turned into a ten-year friendship. Well *whooptie-effing-doo* Catherine! Good for you! Did you read that with a straight face? I tried, I failed! Anyhow, what's the point? Glad you asked! I mentioned in chapter one that we must "Mean WHAT we say, say what WE mean!". That transcends to our day to day behaviors albeit relationships, work life or self-care. Whatever we demonstrate routinely, our kids will come to mimic in their lives. There are exceptions. For the most part, this is as much a golden rule as, "do unto others....".

What makes you tic? What's the one thing that you can't live without? Friendship? Companionship? Money? Entrepreneurship? Purses? God? What's that one thing? How often do you spend time with, working on or for that thing? Why? Being a good parent is the same way. I dare say the relationship with your kids is as important as your relationship with yourself. Your relationship with yourself dictates your relationship with your kids. Stay with me, I promise we're going somewhere!

Do you start and stop? Do you have trouble focusing on anything long enough to finish it? Are you successful in everything you try? Are you risk adverse? Scared to try? Are you a daredevil? Fearless and running towards any challenge? Whichever end of the spectrum you entertain, it's you. Your pattern. Your reputation. What your children see you as. Do you see where we are going? How do you want to be remembered? What's the story that you want told at your funeral? Will it be one that focuses on wishy-washiness and materialism or one filled with accomplishment and faithfulness? Whatever your routine demonstration, that's who you are. That's the lesson that you are teaching your children. Right. Wrong. Indifferent. It's the legacy that you are ingraining in your children's minds.

I am extremely rational. Very rarely will you see me spaz or act out in any type of emotional response. Matter of fact, my calm is so emotionally devastating that you'd wish that I would just cry, scream and throw something. To an extent, it's a very proud accomplishment, unless you are a parent. Can you imagine a house full of assholes? All sarcasm and straight faces, no emotion, ever? Let me introduce you to one of my children, the middle child.

Let's start with how she got to where she is. In chapter one, I introduced you to my ten-year relationship with their father. My pregnancy with their sister introduced me to this thing called feelings. At nineteen, I had plenty, internalized and expressed. I was a psycho in all instances of the word. I had no concept of healthy expression and no one to teach me how to deal with anything felt during those nine months well into the first few years of parenthood. I looked back on how I handled my first pregnancy and determined that my second would be the opposite. Until navigating into my own journey of healthy emotional awareness and intelligence, I did not know that your children experience your realities while you are carrying them. Their delicate emotional states are strongly influenced by that experience. I have one child that is extremely expressive. One that is habitually unbothered and a son that appears to be balanced. We're watching him like a hawk!

The middle child. The intellect. The open minded, free thinking, extremely adamant and grounded in her belief's child. The, *"I feel how I feel, you need to be okay with and respect that feeling because there's no way that you are changing my mind since I am right"*, child. The child that has held school offices, won literary, academic awards and is praised by most of her teachers alike. The child that irritates the fillings in my teeth. Oh, she gets on my last nerve! Theory is her reality. She hasn't had enough life experience to support her strong opinions however, in many cases, her logic is sound. She is bright!

She was well into her teens before I had ever seen her sincerely cry. It was my fault. I prided myself in having it all together. I'm kind of bright too. I've accomplished a few amazing things. I've overcome some interesting obstacles. I never showed the wear and tear. I never showed the feelings behind the losses experienced. I never showed the struggle to buy school supplies or encourage myself after a devasting disappointment. I showed strength and endurance. I never showed feelings. I gave the impression that tears were a sign of weakness and vulnerability was something to be ashamed of. That's how I was raised!

I was a strong woman. An alpha female. I was growing a cabbage patch of children living at each extreme and judging the other because they weren't the same. My middle child taught me to love in the middle. The need to show the reality of parent and womanhood. The healthiness in embracing your feelings and expressing yourself constructively. The fact that everything that you will attempt will not end in success, it will end in a lesson and an opportunity to begin again. My child's future is her "thing". She will fight tooth and nail to accomplish her dreams and she was killing herself. Adding an unnecessary pressure to live up to an imaginary status quo. It was my fault! In whatever we are, we must display consistency in it. Intentionally and unintentionally our children are watching to determine their next.

REFLECTIONS, "BE CONSISTENT!"

BE INTENTIONAL!

There are very few things that happen by accident. The way your life turns out and how your kids grow up are two of those things. You are the glue that holds the future together. God's wrapped all up in it however that's not everyone's belief so for those that live by a different philosophy, we can agree that you are in fact a key factor in how your end is determined. Especially when it comes to your kids.

Proverbs 22:6, "Train up a child in the way he should go, and when he is old he will not depart from it." What does that mean? Discipline is a form of love, if we fail to create a structure for our children, anything will go. If we fail to set a routine of washing hands before a meal and after using the restroom, they'll grow up touching food and others with filthy hands. If we fail to set a precedence that our homes and cars should be well maintained and cleaned, we'll set a standard that it's okay to be grimy and falling apart. Are there exceptions? Absolutely. Children rebel. It doesn't mean that right isn't still right, or the lesson didn't stick. It means that until they decide otherwise, they're rebelling against it. It happens. Plant the healthy seeds, anyway. Plant the positive seeds, anyway. Plant the seeds of discipline, anyway.

Anything that we do with consistency is a seed and has both intended and unintended consequences. What example are you unintentionally setting? Do you fill voids with things or substances? Do you lash out at the wrong people? Do you lash out period? Do you internalize emotions? Repress feelings? Fail to address conflict or disagreements? Did you know the consistency of any of these examples teach your children that you don't value you? That your feelings and opinions aren't things that others should respect? Yes! The things that you do consistently, unintentionally have developmental consequences for your family.

I mentioned in the last chapter that I taught my middle child how to suffer in silence. My need to consistently show strength was a cancer and it needed to be cured. I then intentionally decided to express my thoughts, feelings and insecurities about my relationships, accomplishments and future. I had no choice. The decision had to be a conscious one that I stuck to regardless. My children's lives depended on it. They start to learn how to address the world by what they see in their homes. Read that again. We are their first role models, relationships and heartbreaks. That's a whole lot of pressure. Does that mean that we can't make mistakes? Does that mean that we won't make mistakes? The answer to both is no. You're reading a book about my mistakes, the lessons that I learned in effort of helping you to avoid those and make new ones. Parenting is unchartered territory with on the job training.

The middle child told me that I am not "motherly", I'm to the point and although she feels like she needs that, she appreciates the fact that I am how I am. I'm not changing. As she explained, because she did quickly before I put her out of my car. Serious, not serious. She explained that her friend's moms put you in the mindset of the good-good girlfriend. They will just listen to the tea and move on. I'm not that person. That's not a strength that I possess, nor do I want to grow that trait. We can talk about it, once or twice. I will listen. After that second conversation, we need to start discussing the plan to move forward and secure a path to not experience that again.

None of my children dwell on things, not even the three-year-old. They don't carry grudges or lack forgiveness. Life moves on regardless to whether you want to or not. I have intentionally worked with them to develop that understanding. My greatest fear for my children is that they get, stuck. If that means that I must be transparent in my feelings, so be it. If that means that I must share experiences according their understanding, so be it. My children are not allowed to have an experience that they can not move on from. I have seen it and it's painful. If there is breath in your body, you must move forward. You move forward by dealing with it. Sometimes that is in the very moment. Other times that's a few days later. No matter the time, we all must address and deal with the thing, whatever it is.

You must get over the breakup. You must get over the layoff. You must get over the betrayal. You must get over the failure. You must decide that this will be the last cry. The last time you tell that story. The last time you cringe when you see them. The last time you live inside the box they placed you in. You must make up your mind and then be intentional in developing the right relationships to support your move forward.

I would apologize for giving the impression that this chapter would be consistent with the others. This chapter is the catalyst that moves you from consistency to prioritizing the right relationships. It's all about your decisions.

REFLECTIONS, "BE INTENTIONAL!"

DEMONSTRATE HEALTHY RELATIONSHIPS!

Have you ever stopped and considered the way your relationships show up to your children? Have you ever stopped and considered how your relationships show up, to you? What pattern exists? The role you play in their successes or failures? Have you ever taken a step back and reviewed these intricate parts of your existence with a fine-tooth comb? I have. It has been an interesting journey.

Some of my past relationships showed just how much I didn't value myself. Others showed how little I respected others. When I started getting this right, it made it difficult to ever fall into either of the previous extremes ever again. When we know better, we do better and for those of us who were not taught what healthy looks like growing up, it's a tougher journey to navigate as an adult. It's also even more important that we figure this out so that we can help our babies start on the good foot.

My ten-year relationship with my girls' father was unhealthy. In hindsight it's the same relationship that I had with my mother. How would I have ever known to get out of something that I had been in my entire life? Who was supposed to explain this to me? Their dad isn't a bad person, neither is my mom, they're just not right for me. Can you relate?

What made the relationships unhealthy? Dare I say, toxic. Any relationship that is one sided or seemingly codependent is unhealthy. If a relationship negatively triggers you, it's toxic. There's a level of responsibility that we must take as well. If you willingly stay in a relationship that does any of the above, you must address your own toxicity. I stayed, for ten years. I enabled my mom, for decades. At no point was I a victim, I was a willing participant in everything that I experienced. Until I opted to distance myself or completely sever the ties, I can safely say that my continued suffering was no one's fault but my own. No one can repeatedly mistreat you without permission. My acceptance and owning of that one thing helped to start my healing and identifying what healthy looks like.

I knew that these weren't relationships that I ever wanted for my kids so after taking the first step of removing myself from the romantic relationship, I started dealing with me and my why's. Once I identified what damaged me in my relationship with my mother, I made sure that I was not that person to my own children. I also never spoke negatively about either of them until my children got to a point where they brought things to my attention. They love their father and grandmother. They have always and will continue to have relationships with them both, absent of my involvement. I stay in my lane. My opinion about them is mute.

I've had challenges with my own father as well, my bottom line and behavior is consistent. My parents had rough upbringings. To an extent, their stories aren't mine to tell. I can say that no one taught either to be a parent or love and they both did the best that they could with what they had. Ultimately, I turned out decent. I had to own a lot and be intentional about everything that plagued me emotionally, but I made it out okay. My goal is to ensure that my kids don't have to unpack anything emotionally except the things they or life brings on. The foundation has been laid for them to approach relationships with open eyes and full hearts.

I made my exit and started looking for what looks right in other relationships. This is the only time that I would ever advise looking at someone else's life as a model. All relationships are different and require different things to make them work. Success for each couple is weighed on a different scale, it's very personal. However, there are core things that should exist in every relationship, the rest is a la cart. Respect. Trust. Fidelity. Friendship. Outside platonic friendships. Guys/Girls night out is required! Provision. Protection. You must like each other. You must be genuinely attracted to each other. Traditionally healthy relationships aren't explained. We may see couples that have existed for twenty plus years, but no one tells us how they stayed in love. Did you notice that I never listed love? That was intentional. Love is implied by the existence of all those things and no couple is naturally in love forever. They work at it. They choose it.

I believe strongly in the laws of attraction. When I started healing, right relationships came into my life as positive examples. Being close to both the husband and wife allowed me the opportunity to see both sides. Being in a failed relationship allowed me to grow in my current one of seven years. It's not a fairytale. It's worth the effort and that's the reality of relationships. They are work!

Romantic. Platonic. Familial. Any relationship worth having is going to stretch and test you. What they shouldn't do are deplete and diminish you. If you're consistently pouring, never being filled, get out. If you're consistently wondering and confused, get out. If you're consistently in a negative space, get out. The right relationships don't test your peace, they test your sanity.

REFLECTIONS,
"DEMONSTRATE HEALTHY RELATIONSHIPS!"

WORK THE JOB, DON'T LET IT WORK YOU!

Work-life balance isn't a myth, it's a requirement. Unfortunately, it's not something that you ever master because it doesn't exist. What? That doesn't make sense! What do you mean? Well, it doesn't exist. Life will always be imbalanced at some point. There'll be opportunities to spend more time with family and less at work. Then, there'll be occurrences where work will take precedence and family will have to take a back seat. The key is to not have too many instances where one is receiving the bulk of the attention.

What you do for a living, to provide for your family is important because it's how you keep the lights on, cover the roof you live under and buy school supplies. When you die, your job will replace you, within 90 days. Your family can not. *We can't become so consumed with making a living that we neglect making a life.* I'm certain someone else said that first, I unfortunately don't know who so for the sake of not plagiarizing, italics have been added. Let's move on!

When I was twenty-two and pregnant with my youngest daughter, I had the opportunity of a lifetime. If you were raised by baby boomers, like I was, what I am about to share is the epitome of the American Dream. I started a job as a Customer Service Agent at Chicago Transit Authority, within six months to a year, I was a full-time Rapid Transit Operator. If you know anything about city jobs and blue-collar work, you know that they pay very well, are union and most people retire from these companies. At twenty-two with two children and no college degree, this was a dream come true.

Let's backup, I mentioned that I was pregnant at nineteen, I didn't mention that I was also entering my sophomore year at Pennsylvania State University – McKeesport Campus as the President of Student Government, majoring in Computer Engineering. I never returned to PSU nor served a day as President, instead I took heed to my dad's ultimatum. My father vehemently disapproved of my pregnancy and of course, who I opted to become pregnant by. His idea of support in the situation was to play my future against itself. My dad had a child at nineteen, worked his way through college and experienced the struggle firsthand. That's not the life he wanted for me. With a straight face, he said," *I'll continue to pay for school if you have an abortion!*" Twenty years, three children, two degrees and three businesses later, what do you think I chose? Better yet, who do you think I chose?

As an RTO for CTA, the hours were plentiful, the benefits were amazing, and the pay was a blessing. I was able to provide for my children without issue. I just never saw my newborn or toddler outside of drop off in the morning and pickup at night. I worked 3rd shift. I was new to the company, so I bounced from terminal to terminal and had very little control over my schedule. I eventually hit a wall, literally and figuratively. I had an accident on my train, my brakes failed and although no lives were lost or injuries were reported, I was never the same.

I returned to my previous job as an office assistant for Coldwell Banker and made a life changing declaration, I'd never work for a company that I felt didn't value me first and support my being present for my children. I'm a mother before anything and after that 2.5-year experience at CTA, I never wavered in that position. Has it been easy to stick to this principle? Yes and no. Yes, because I am a better employee in environments that value family. No, because it limited me to certain positions for a season. I did what I had to do and worked the positions that I needed to work to eventually get to where I have been for the last few years. My last three positions prioritized family and me to a point where I had the flexibility to maneuver as needed.

I won't paint the picture that this is something that can be accomplished simply, I have two degrees, work in my degree fields and have busted my behind to get to where I am. I took demotions. I started over. I have truly struggled. It was worth it to me. My peace of mind is invaluable, and my family is my priority. Every decision was a means to be able to support the things I value most, I made sacrifices where I needed to. I kept first things first. Be honest with yourself. Figure out your plan to ensure that your values are not compromised, that you can peacefully get to your end game. As an employee, someone else is building their dream, at your expense. That isn't a bad thing, unless your suffering while doing the work.

REFLECTIONS,
"WORK THE JOB, DON'T LET IT WORK YOU!"

INCORPORATE! THAT'S IT!

You will not create generational wealth unless you invest in something outside your employer's dream. Let me scream this for the people in the back. It will not happen! The rat race is a real thing! Living paycheck to paycheck is a poverty trap. You owe your children better than what you experienced.

Does this mean that you must be the next Mark Zuckerberg, Bill Gates, Jay Z or Walton Family? Absolutely not! It does mean that you should turn your passion into a profit and build something that can generate both passive and aggressive income. Real estate investment. Authoring books. Apparel lines. Consulting. Anything that provides a service and a dollar for that service is the topic at hand.

How do I do that? I have no idea where to start. Everything you need to know about business startup, entrepreneurship, intrapreneurship and solopreneurship is available for free on the US Small Business Administration website (sba.gov). If long reads aren't necessarily your "thing", here's the quick steps and then we're moving on:

Find your passion. Identify what keeps you up at night and what service you'd provide for free that solves a problem. For me, I have a soft spot for career development and single mothers thriving. I now offer services to support both arenas in several ways.

After you find your passion, obtain your tax/employer identification number. This number is a social security number for businesses, and it classifies you as a sole proprietorship, limited liability company, corporation or not for profit. Based on the classification, your next steps vary.

Register your business with your local secretary of state and in some cases, attorney general. Lastly, open your business checking accounts, websites and social media. Walking through each step helps you to prepare for the next. It's time consuming and costly. It's also the greatest investment you'll ever make in yours and your family's future.

REFLECTIONS, "INCORPORATE! THAT'S IT!"

FIND THE MUSTARD SEED, WATCH IT GROW!

We've discussed six of the seven steps to keep your sanity and be a GREAT leader in your home; none of them are possible without this last one. *"If you believe it, you can achieve it!"* *"Whether you can or can't is both true!"* *"All you have to do, is believe…"* NO matter what mantra you live by or cliché you turn to, the only way that you will ever move from step A to step B is by faith. A belief that you can. The positivity to try.

I started my collegiate journey with good intentions and doing everything right. I graduated from high school with honors. Got accepted into a division one university. Ended my freshman year with honors. Joined clubs and won a seat on the student council. I got pregnant and chose my oldest daughter throwing everything that I had accomplished out the window.

Choosing a child with no education, occupation or marriage was a guarantee for welfare, poverty and generational struggle. That was the consensus. No one believed that I would bounce back from this. 2.5-years later when I had my second daughter, although I was enrolled in school and working, the light dimly shined. I was making my life up as I went along. I had no idea how I would survive and raise those girls. I just knew that failure wasn't an option and my children ultimately had no one to rely on but me.

Everything accomplished was done in both faith and fear. Those two f's have walked hand and hand my entire life. If it didn't terrify me, I didn't try it. In my gut I knew that the task wasn't big enough. I told you chapters ago that I was a psycho, this is a trait. Seriously, there's a good and bad (ying and yang) to everything. I discovered my emotions while pregnant, I also discovered my passion for success an inability to quit. Doing well is a major driving force in my life, my children gave me something greater than myself to be successful for. Do it afraid! Whatever it is that sits on your heart. When you look from left to right, you know that this isn't it. What's holding you back? Fear? We all have it. Failure? We all have and will continually fail. My greatest accomplishments have been born out of failures.

Each time you step out on faith and try despite your circumstances, naysayers and finances, you become stronger and stronger. Do it afraid! Your future is counting on you growing through your past!

REFLECTIONS,
"FIND THE MUSTARD SEED, WATCH IT GROW!"

ABOUT THE AUTHOR

An IO Psychologist by trade, Catherine McNeil has earned her Bachelor of Business Administration and a Master of Arts in Industrial/Organizational Psychology with almost two decades of experience and applied knowledge from management and leadership roles inside a myriad of arenas. But these aren't her greatest accomplishments!! As a young parent of two teen daughters and a toddler aged son, Catherine has an equal affinity for developing young adults into our future leaders. Currently, she is the Founder of CHBM Services, a career an employee development consultancy and CHBM Services Development Programming L3C. Her latest project creates the materials for and facilitates career development workshops for Single Working Mother's between the ages of 18-40 years of age. Formerly, her role included the design, implementation and administration, of a 90-day Cohort Job Training program that serviced at-risk African American youth ages 18-30. As the Career Development Manager in an Austin Community based not-for-profit on Chicago's West side, Catherine was responsible for training young adults in areas of Job Preparedness, Personal Growth and Development.

The CHBM Services LLC body of businesses & products are dedicated to reducing poverty among single parent homes by providing reduced cost services to individuals and entities requiring Career Development Support.

    CHBM Services Website: https://www.chbmservices.com/

    SMNPCE INC Website: https://www.smnpceinc.org/

THANK YOU FOR READING!

1. Please leave a review on amazon!
2. Pick up A Mother's Love; 31 days of Affirmations for Single Mothers for a mom you know!
3. Join the FB group, Single Mother's Navigating Parenting | Careers | Entrepreneurship INC!